# ATTACK OF THE LIVING MASK

## titles in Large-Print Editions:

# CHOOSE YOUR OWN NIGHTMARE #17

## ATTACK OF THE LIVING MASK

*by Robert Hirschfeld*

*Illustrated by Bill Schmidt*

An Edward Packard Book

Gareth Stevens Publishing
MILWAUKEE

For a free color catalog describing Gareth Stevens' list of high-quality books and multimedia programs, call 1-800-542-2595 (USA) or 1-800-461-9120 (Canada). Gareth Stevens Publishing's Fax: (414) 225-0377. See our catalog, too, on the World Wide Web: http://gsinc.com

**Library of Congress Cataloging-in-Publication Data**

Hirschfeld, Robert, 1942-
    Attack of the living mask / by Robert Hirschfeld ; illustrated by Bill Schmidt.
       p. cm. — (Choose your own nightmare; #17)
    Summary: The reader controls the action in this story about several young people who go looking for a missing friend on Halloween night.
    ISBN 0-8368-2074-6 (lib. bdg.)
    1. Plot-your-own stories. [1. Halloween—Fiction. 2. Horror stories.
3. Plot-your-own stories.] I. Schmidt, Bill, ill. II. Title. III. Series.
PZ7.H59794At   1998
[Fic]—dc21                                     97-41910

This edition first published in 1998 by
**Gareth Stevens Publishing**
1555 North RiverCenter Drive, Suite 201
Milwaukee, Wisconsin 53212 USA

Printed in the United States of America

1 2 3 4 5 6 7 8 9 02 01 00 99 98

# ATTACK OF THE LIVING MASK

# WARNING!

You have probably read books where scary things happen to people. Well, in *Choose Your Own Nightmare*, you're right in the middle of the action. The scary things are happening to you!

You and your friends were ready to hit the neighborhood streets and load up on candy, but this Halloween night turns out a little differently than you'd expected. . . .

Don't forget—YOU control your fate. Only you can decide what happens. Follow the instructions at the bottom of each page. The thrills and chills that happen to you will depend on your choices!

Halloween comes only once a year. You don't want to miss a single minute of it . . . or do you? Find out whether this book is full of tricks or treats on page 1 . . . and *CHOOSE YOUR OWN NIGHTMARE!*

*"YA-A-H-H-W-O-O-O-O-O-O-O-O-H-R-R-R!"*

The howl is loud enough to break your eardrums. You poke Timmy Fitch in the ribs.

"Quit it!" you tell him.

*"Ow!* You dented my costume!" Timmy rubs the spot. "It's Halloween, remember? Plus, there's a full moon!"

"You're a robot, not a werewolf," says Jordan Stone, adjusting her halo. "Robots don't howl at the moon."

"Maybe he's a robot werewolf." Annie Kidman giggles through her lizard mask.

You're trick-or-treating with your friends. You're dressed as a red Magic Marker. You wish you hadn't let your mom talk you into it. Timmy keeps asking if you're supposed to be a candle.

"Maybe there's brownies," says Annie when you arrive at the Farrell house. "I *love* Mrs. Farrell's brownies!"

Jeff Farrell was supposed to be with you, but he never showed up.

"I bet Jeff's waiting here," you say, ringing the doorbell.

Mr. and Mrs. Farrell open the door.

*Go to the next page.*

# 2

"*Trick or treat!*" you yell.

"Where's Jeff?" Mrs. Farrell asks. "He said he'd be with you."

You look at your friends. None of you knows.

"When did you see Jeff last?" asks Mr. Farrell.

"At school," Annie says. Everyone nods.

"Not since then?" Mrs. Farrell sounds upset.

"He may be going around alone," you say, hoping this will make her feel better. But you don't believe it's true.

Mrs. Farrell shakes her head. "He hasn't called, and he didn't come home for dinner."

"Listen, kids," says Mr. Farrell. "If you see Jeff, tell him to get home *fast,* Halloween or no Halloween. All right?"

"Sure," Timmy says. He looks worried.

The Farrells close their door as you leave.

"Where do you think he is?" Jordan asks.

You shrug. "Beats me."

"I think *I* know." You can hardly hear Timmy's voice, and he's looking at his feet.

"What do you mean?" demands Jordan.

*Find out on page 3.*

"At lunch, Jeff said he was going to Graystone Pond after school," Timmy mumbles.

"Why didn't you tell his parents?" you exclaim. "They're worried!"

"I don't want to get him in trouble," Timmy says. No one wants their kids at Graystone Pond. You don't like going there anyway. It's too creepy.

Once the pond was okay to swim and fish in. But someone dumped chemicals in it. The fish died. You'd be crazy to swim there now. And there are stories about Graystone Pond, scary ones. About someone—or some*thing*—lurking out there. . . .

"I wouldn't go down there if you *paid* me," Annie declares.

"But that's exactly what Jeff *would* do," you say. Jeff is always doing crazy things. He loves to frighten people.

"Jeff is in trouble," Timmy says. "And I know what we have to do!" He drops his treat bag. "Let's go look for him! He said he was going to the pond—"

*The pond? Oh no. Turn to page 58.*

# 4

"We won't be hungry for long. Now there's enough food here for all of us!" one of the creatures shrieks. It jumps on Annie's back and sinks its fangs into her shoulder.

"Get off me!" Annie screams in terror. To your surprise, another creature pulls the first one off and throws it, squealing, across the room.

"Wait your turn!" snarls one of the creatures. You think it's Marty. "There's plenty to go around! Take these two away until we're ready to begin the feast!"

Two creatures grab Annie's arms and pull. "I'll take this one myself," Marty declares.

He grabs for you, but you dodge aside. A few of the others try to get you, but you twist away. There's nothing between you and the open door! You can run for it!

"*Help! Help me!*" You look back. Annie is being carried out of the room.

---

*If you want to try to be a hero, turn to page 34.*

*If you don't want to risk being the monsters' Halloween dinner, turn to page 73.*

"We *have* to go through this tunnel," you insist. "We'll never get away from the vampires here in the cave." You feel a breeze blowing out of the mouth of the tunnel. "This is an exit! I know it is!"

"But I'll get stuck!" Annie says.

"No you won't," you tell her. "I'll be right there with you."

Annie chews her lip.

"Okay," she whispers. "But don't leave me alone."

Annie crawls into the narrow opening. You follow behind her. The tunnel walls and roof press down on you. But you keep going.

"Keep going, Annie," you encourage her. "We'll be out soon."

You don't hear any noise behind you. Maybe the vampires are too big to use the tunnel.

"The breeze is getting colder. We must be nearly out!" you shout.

"Here it is!" Annie cries with relief. "The opening! I'm outside!"

She helps pull you up. You suck in cool air, happy not to have that rock pressing down on you anymore.

*Turn to page 63.*

"Jeff Farrell," you answer. "He was supposed to meet us, and we can't find him."

"Oh," the kid says. "Jeff *Farrell.* Yeah, we saw him."

"About fifteen minutes ago," says his friend.

"Right," a third kid agrees. "He was at the party. He's probably still there."

Annie's eyes light up. "What party?"

"The big Halloween party," the first kid says. "Didn't Jeff tell you about it?"

"No," you say angrily. "Where is it?"

"Cedar Street," says the first kid. "We're going back there. Come with us."

You frown. "Cedar Street? That's far."

"Just a few blocks," says one of the kids.

"I don't know . . . ," you say, looking at Annie. "My mom said to stay close to home."

"C'mon," the first kid urges. "There's cool music . . ."

"And lots of kids . . . ," adds another.

"There's great stuff to eat! Candy, cake, ice cream . . . ," says a third kid.

---

*Skip the party? Turn to page 17.*

*Go to the party with Annie? Turn to page 29.*

You all squeeze outside and shut the window behind you.

"Uh-oh," says Jeff. "We've got company."

Ms. Venner floats in the air in front of you. Behind her are several other witches, some women and some men.

"Three of you," says Ms. Venner. "We wanted more, but it's late. Three is enough. Prepare them for the sacrifice."

"As you command," says a male witch.

Annie tries to run, but a male witch grabs her. Others take you and Jeff. The blond witch holding you has a grip like steel. Her fingernails cut into your arms.

"If you fight, you'll be sorry," she snarls.

The three of you are taken from the parking lot to a grove of old trees. In the center of a clearing in the woods lies a flat stone. On the stone is a long knife with a gleaming blade.

"Let their blood be spilled," says Ms. Venner. She picks up the knife and points to you. You're carried to the stone.

*Turn to page 30.*

**8**

But Jeff isn't laughing. In fact, he looks scared. The tape player is lying on the ground at his feet.

"I didn't do that," he says.

"Yeah, right," Jordan says.

*A-A-A-A-O-O-O-R-R-R-G-H!*

You see that the cassette player is turned off. *"Shhh!* Listen!" Jeff whispers.

Everyone is very quiet. Something is crashing through the bushes and growling.

"Run! Let's get out of here!" Jeff yells.

"Run where?" you ask. "If that thing wants to hurt us, it'll catch us in the woods."

"Let's hide in the shack," Annie says.

"That thing will rip the shack apart!" Jeff yells.

"Yeah," says Timmy, "but if it catches us in the woods, it'll rip *us* apart. I say we try the shack!"

"We're near the pond," Jeff replies. "Maybe we can get to the island in the middle."

The growling is very close. What should you do?

---

*Try to outrun the thing on page 22.*

*If you'd rather hide in the shack, turn to page 16.*

"How did you get away?" you ask.

"I climbed out a window. I don't think they know I'm gone yet."

"If they took Annie to the cellar, they'll know you're gone now," you tell him.

Jeff looks scared. "We have to run for it!"

You look around, panicked. "Where? I don't know where we are, or how to get out of here!"

"I do!" Jeff says. "Come on!"

He starts running—and you're right behind him. If there are any people around, they're all in their houses, and the lights are out. You're lucky there's a full moon, so you don't trip over anything.

Jeff turns some corners and cuts across empty lots. "How far do we have to go?" you call.

"Just a few minutes, and—" He stops suddenly. "Listen! You hear that?"

At first you hear nothing. Then your blood turns cold.

Not far away, something is howling. Other howls join in . . . and they're getting louder!

*They're after you, and they're closing in!*

*Turn to page 47 fast, before they get you!*

"Jeff?" asks Annie's trembly voice.

"No. It's me," you tell her. *"Quiet!"*

*THUMP, THUMP, THUMP, THUMP.*

The footsteps are closer. You lie still, hardly breathing. Maybe it won't see you.

"Who's in my house?" asks a voice. "Who's come to visit on Halloween?"

"Mommy and Daddy can't come to the door," says another voice. "They're not well." The voice giggles. "In fact, Mommy and Daddy have gone to pieces!"

You gasp. Could it be . . . ?

Two young men stand a few feet away. They're dressed in old-fashioned clothes: suits and ties. Although it's dark, their skin seems to glow. Their faces are twisted and crazy-looking, and their eyes are wide and staring. They don't blink. The young men smile at you. Both of them carry axes.

You rub your eyes and look again.

Drops of dark liquid fall from the blades. Razor-sharp blades.

You feel as if you're about to faint from fear.

"It's *them,*" Jeff whispers excitedly. "The Caswell ghosts!"

*Yikes! Hurry to page 33!*

## 12

Close to you, you can see bushes moving. "Look!" you say. "Whatever it is, here it comes!"

Annie jumps up to run, but Jordan grabs her.

You point your flashlight at the bushes as something crashes through and stops in front of you. It's Jeff!

Jeff stares at you and your friends. You stare back.

"What are you doing here?" he asks.

"We came to rescue you," Jordan tells him. "What are *you* doing here?"

"Yeah!" Annie demands. "Aside from scaring us to death!"

Jeff puts a finger to his lips. *"Shhh!"* He's carrying a portable cassette player.

"What's that for?" you ask.

"Listen," Jeff says. He pushes a button. Hideous howling booms from the speaker.

*"You!"* Jordan says.

Jeff smirks. "I got this scary sound effects tape at the mall."

*Go to page 64.*

You scramble out from under the table, keeping it between you and the ghost. You hope you don't trip and fall. If you do, the ghost will get you for sure.

A moment later, you hear Jeff scream. *"No! Don't! A-A-A-A-H-H!"* His voice is cut off by a sickening *thud.*

"It killed Jeff!" Annie screams.

As you back away, watching the ghost, Annie screams again.

"Look out behind you!"

You look over your shoulder. The other ghost is there, holding a big bucket in one hand and a flickering lantern in the other. With its weird glow and hideous face, it looks even more horrible than the one chasing you. On the floor in front of the ghost lies Jeff, covered with bloodstains. You stop, afraid to move.

You can't believe you're staring at Jeff's corpse! Jeff is dead! Are you going to die, too?

"You're still here?" the ghost near you asks. "Good! Your friend is no fun anymore. His blood is in this bucket, and when we're done with you, yours will be, too."

---

*A bloodbath? Ugh. Turn to page 69.*

**14**

"There's a Halloween party at Glenwood Middle School. Let's go there," Annie suggests.

Jeff nods. "Yeah. Why not? At least it'll be safe."

You agree. "If we see any ghosts there, they'll be kids we know."

The front doors and halls of the school are covered with decorations: cutout paper jack-o'-lanterns, bats, pointy witch hats, broomsticks. As you go in, a grown-up in a Dracula costume and fangs waves at you. After a minute you realize it's Mr. James, your science teacher. Other teachers and some bigger kids in costumes direct you to the cafeteria.

The cafeteria is full of costumed kids. There's a big space cleared for dancing, and rock music mixed with recordings of wolf howls and screams is blasting. At one end of the room stands a snack table with a big punch bowl.

Annie spots the refreshments. "All *right!*" she says, making a beeline for the table.

Jeff looks around and sighs. "This is going to be totally boring!"

*Is it? Turn to page 39.*

The old man puts down the rag and glass. "What brings you out here?" he says. "We were just about to close, but Martha made a pumpkin pie, and there's some nice hot cider—"

"No, thanks," Annie says.

The woman looks closely at your faces. "Is something wrong?"

"Can we help?" asks the old man.

You exchange glances with Annie. You're sorry you came in here. These people are nice, but they won't be able to do anything for you, and you may have gotten them into danger.

"Can we use your phone?" you ask quickly.

"You certainly could . . . ," the woman says, and you smile hopefully. "If we had one, that is. But we don't."

"Used to," says the old man, "but we never used it much, so we had it taken out ten years ago."

"No, Henry," the woman corrects him, "it was twelve years ago. The year we had that terrible rainstorm."

"I believe you're right," the man answers.

"We'd better go," Annie says nervously.

You peer out the door. "They're coming!"

---

*Hurry to page 36.*

# 16

You hear heavy footsteps and panting near the edge of the clearing. There's no time to lose. "Into the shack! Quick!" you yell, racing for the door.

"What if the hermit doesn't want company?" Annie says, running beside you.

"Then we're in trouble," you say.

As you reach the door, you glance back over your shoulder. A big, furry creature is standing behind a tree, looking at you with gleaming yellow eyes. You yank at the rope handle on the door . . . and it opens! Everyone piles inside, even Jeff. You slam the door shut. Then you shine your flashlights around. There isn't much to see.

"Hello?" calls Timmy. "Anyone home?"

No one answers.

"Hey, Jeff," you say. "Guess you weren't scaring anybody, after all. The hermit is out."

"Maybe he's trick-or-treating," Annie says. "I wish *I* was."

There's a loud *thump* against the wall of the shack. You hear fierce growling and snarling.

Something smashes the door. The old planks shake.

---

*What is it? Go to page 28.*

"We should just stick around here," you whisper to Annie. "That party's too far—and we don't know these guys."

Annie pouts. "But I can't go by myself!" She gives you a pleading look. "We won't stay if it's not fun."

But your mind is made up. "Sorry," you say firmly.

Annie sighs and watches the strangers leave without you. "Thanks a lot."

"We can hit some other houses," you suggest.

Annie's face brightens. "Okay. Let's go to Mrs. Reynolds'! She gives great candy."

On the way to Mrs. Reynolds' house, you pass an empty lot overgrown with bushes and weeds. Annie stops short.

"Listen!" she says, frowning.

You stop. "What?"

"I heard something moving."

"I don't hear anything," you say.

But as you start walking, you *do* hear a movement behind you. Suddenly someone leaps on your back!

You buck and twist, trying to get them off.

*Find out what has you on page 80.*

# 18

"Let's go," you tell Jeff. "Annie went to your haunted house, didn't she?"

"Aren't you getting hot in that mask?" you ask Annie as you head down the school steps.

Annie shrugs. "I'm okay."

The new kid smiles. "Well, I'm sure hot!"

He reaches behind his head and pulls. To your horror, his face peels off! Underneath, he's green and scaly, with slitted yellow eyes— just like Annie's mask. A forked tongue flicks out of his mouth, along with big yellow drops of slime. The thing tosses you his human mask.

"You're awesomely cute," the thing says to Annie. "I really like you!"

"I . . . I'm not—" Annie drops her treat bag and runs away. The monster chases her. "Wait!" it calls. "Come back!"

You and Jeff watch, astonished.

"Hey, guys?" a voice says. You look down. The monster's human-face mask is talking! "Where can I get some arms and legs and a body like yours? They're really cool!"

**The End**

# 20

"You think this will work?" Annie whispers.

"I sure hope so," you answer.

The monster sees you and springs forward. *"Charge!"*

You and Annie lunge for it, the umbrella held like a spear. The point pierces the beast's stomach. You maintain your grip as it sinks in deep. The monster screams in pain and tries to pull the pole out, but you keep pushing. Finally the monster topples down the stairs, blood pouring from its wound.

The other beasts back away. The injured monster tries one last time to get the pole out of its body, and then slumps over. It's dead!

Shrieking in fear, the smaller creatures run, falling over each other to escape. A minute later, you and Annie are alone in the house.

"Why did they run away like that?" she asks.

"We killed their leader," you explain. "They're afraid of us!"

Annie giggles. "Cool!"

"Let's get out of here," you say.

"You think it's safe?" Annie asks.

"Yeah," you reply. "I do."

You *are* safe—for this Halloween, anyway.

**The End**

"Not the shack!" you say. "We could get trapped in there."

"The pond!" Jeff shouts.

You all take off. Behind you something races into the clearing. You hear another howl.

"Faster!" Jeff yells.

You try to keep up, but tree branches get in your way, as if they want to trap you. You hear something smashing through the woods, snarling and growling.

"Ahhh!" You hear a loud scream, which stops suddenly. Who was it?

"There it is!" Jeff pants. A second later, you're standing next to him, gasping for breath, at the edge of Graystone Pond. The awful noises behind you have stopped. The other kids come up. Everyone but Timmy.

"Where's Timmy?" you ask.

Jordan catches her breath. "He tripped and fell and this . . . *monster* came and I ran away."

"What kind of monster?" Jeff asks.

Jordan is shaking. "Like a man, but with a wolf head!"

You hear another howl.

"Here it comes again!" says Annie.

*Turn to page 55.*

"Who are these guys?" you ask Jeff.

"My cousins, Ernie and Joey," Jeff replies. "Their dad does TV and movie special effects—space aliens, monsters, stuff like that. Their family just bought this house."

"What about the Caswells?" Annie asks suspiciously. "Did you make that up, too?"

"Uh-uh," Jeff says. "It's true. They really chopped up their folks."

"But Dad doesn't believe in ghosts, so he bought the house anyway," Ernie says. "He got us the black light, the costumes, even the fake blood." He points to the bucket.

"Your dad helped you do this?" you ask.

"Well, um . . . he didn't know my plan, exactly . . . ," Jeff mumbles.

"It was a dumb idea," Joey says.

Jeff shrugs. "Hey! It's Halloween. You're supposed to scare people."

"Sorry we scared you," Ernie tells you.

"Jeff said it'd be funny," Joey adds. "He said you'd laugh about it afterward."

*Feel like laughing? Turn to page 77.*

## 24

"I'll go with you," you tell Timmy. You don't really want to go to Graystone Pond at night, but if Jeff really is in trouble, you feel you have to help.

"I know he's in danger," Timmy insists.

Annie looks scared. "Okay, I'm in," she says finally. "But you guys better not tell my parents where we were tonight, or I'll be grounded till I'm forty!"

"It's going to be totally dark out there," says Jordan. "We need flashlights."

"I have one." Timmy pulls a small flashlight from his pocket. "It's pretty good, too."

"My house is on the way," you say. "We can get more flashlights there."

You borrow flashlights for everyone from your garage, sneaking away before your parents see you. You don't like doing this, but it may be a matter of life or death.

You hope it isn't *your* life or death.

*Turn to page 56.*

"We can stop the truck," Annie says, racing toward the road with you on her heels. She dashes out into the middle of the road and holds up her hands.

"Don't mention vampires," you say. "They won't believe you."

The truck brakes to a stop, and the driver rolls down his window. "Is something wrong?"

Annie nods. "Yeah, some big guys are chasing us. We need to get away."

The driver peers into the field. "You kids hop in back and hide under that canvas there. We'll get you away from here in a jiffy. Just make room for yourselves among the groceries."

You scramble into the back of the truck and squirm under the canvas, making room among the big packages already there. The truck speeds ahead with a roar.

"Where are we headed?" Annie wonders.

You try to get more comfortable among the bumpy packages. "Into town, I guess."

The truck turns left sharply, and then right.

A few minutes later, the truck stops. The driver calls, "You can come out now."

---

*Turn to page 37.*

## 26

Holding Annie, the man enters the room, followed by another man. Their faces are bloodless and their skin is peeling away. Their eyes stare blankly ahead.

They aren't breathing.

Jeff gasps. "The living dead! They're *ghouls*! This *is* the Ghoul Room!"

The second ghoul goes after Jeff as the first looks at Annie and licks its lips. It opens its mouth to take a bite of her arm.

How can you stop it? You grab a fire extinguisher on the wall. Aiming it at the ghoul holding Annie, you squeeze the handle. A white stream shoots into the ghoul's mouth.

The creature drops Annie and grabs its throat. A moment later, it comes toward you.

"Quick, let's go up those stairs!" shouts Jeff, running from the other ghoul.

*"No!"* screams Annie. "We'll be trapped!"

"But we're trapped *here*!" Jeff yells.

---

*If you want to try the stairs to the windows, turn to page 81.*

*If you'd rather take your chances where you are, turn to page 42.*

"That's nonsense!" snaps the janitor.

"We were locked in there!" you tell them.

Ms. Venner bites her lip. "I thought this was the Ghoul Room. I'm new here, and—"

"Oh, all right," the janitor grumbles. "Halloween's just a big nuisance!"

"The Ghoul Room is closed for the evening," Ms. Venner says as you leave.

"I certainly *hope* so," Annie mutters.

In the cafeteria, the food is all gone.

"Some Halloween *this* was," Jeff whines.

"I'm hungry," says Annie through her lizard mask.

"Why don't you come trick-or-treating with me?" It's a boy your age, smiling at Annie. He's not wearing a costume. "We'll get lots of good stuff."

"Not me," Jeff says. "No way."

"Come on," Annie pleads, looking from you to Jeff.

"*You* decide," Jeff says to you.

---

*If you let Annie have her way, turn to page 18.*

*If you don't want to go, turn to page 78.*

**28**

"Lock the door!" calls Jordan.

You run over to the door. "There *is* no lock."

"I want to get out of here!" Jeff screams. "Right now!"

"Be my guest," you say. "If you want to take your chances with . . . whatever's out there, go on. Maybe the rest of us can get away while it's eating you."

Jeff stays where he is.

*WHAM!* Something slams into the door again.

"I bet the hermit was doing something outside and that thing got him," Timmy says.

"Shut up, Timmy," Jordan says.

*A-A-O-O-O-O-W-W-W-R-R-H!*

The howl comes from right outside, loud enough to shake the whole shack. You hear more snarling, and something hits the door so hard that one of the planks splits down the middle.

*Turn to page 53.*

The strange kids walk fast, and you have to hurry to keep up. "Do you go to Glenwood?" you ask. That's where you and your friends go to school.

The first kid shakes his head. He doesn't slow down. "Uh-uh. We, uh, we go to a private school."

"Which one?" you ask.

"You never heard of it," says a different kid, as you cross a street and turn a corner. "It's not around here."

You're almost running now, and it's hard to keep up. "So why are you in this neighborhood?" you ask, gasping for breath.

"We like it here," says the first kid. "By the way, my name is Marty." You notice he's not breathing hard at all. In fact, he is speeding up. "C'mon, we're almost there!"

You don't know where you are. The full moon throws some light, but you don't like what you see. It's nothing like your neighborhood, that's for sure. You want to find out more about these new kids, but you have to save your breath and energy to keep going at their pace.

---

*Don't get lost! Hurry up and turn to page 46.*

## 30

"No! You can't do this!" You try to pull free, but the witches are too strong. They lay you flat on your back on the stone and hold you down.

"Let me go! I'm just a kid! You'll be in big trouble if you get caught," you say, hoping to scare them.

"Tonight, demons and witches rule," says Ms. Venner.

*"Cut their throats! Spill their blood,"* chant the others.

"Let their blood run bright and red," says Ms. Venner as she raises the knife.

It's no use trying to reason with them.

You swallow. Your life flashes in front of you. Just as Ms. Venner's about to slash your throat, you hear the barking of a dog.

Annoyed, Ms. Venner lowers the knife. You twist your head. A medium-size dog is standing a few feet away, barking furiously at the witches.

"Kill that dog!" Ms. Venner mutters. Two other witches run to obey. But new voices can be heard. They're close by—and getting closer.

*Turn to page 45.*

# 32

You stay in the boat. Reluctantly, Annie joins you. You and Jeff each grab an oar. Jeff gives the boat a shove off the bottom of the pond, and you start to row.

Annie bends over the side to stare down at the water. The boat tilts.

"Sit in the middle!" you shout. "You'll tip us over!"

Annie sits still as you move away from shore. The full moon gives you plenty of light.

*"Look!"* Jordan points to the shore.

You spot an animal. Or is it a man? It stands on its hind legs, but it has a long snout and pointed ears. Its eyes glow yellow in the moonlight, and it sniffs and moves its head around.

*"Quiet!"* hisses Jeff. "Maybe it won't see us."

You shake as the beast roars. You row harder.

"Let it roar," Jeff says. "We're safe now—unless that thing can swim. We'll stay on the island until it's light and—"

*Turn to page 43.*

One of the ghostly young men looks at Jeff and scowls. "Who are you? You know who we are, but we don't know you." The ghost raises its ax high. "It doesn't matter. Let's have some fun!" It lunges forward, the ax over its head.

*"No! Get away!"* Jeff screams. He turns and runs, with the ghost chasing after him.

"Now it's your turn," the other ghost says to you. It starts forward, its ax pointed straight at you.

"Watch out!" Annie yells.

You back away but bump into a table. The ghost laughs. "Now I've got you!"

It swings its ax, aiming for your neck. You duck, and the ax whooshes over your head. Before the ghost can try again, you scramble under the table you just banged into.

"No! I'm too young to die!" someone screams. You jerk back. It sounded like Jeff! You start to sweat. Would the ghosts actually kill him?

Before you can move, Annie calls your name. "We need to get help. This way!" she shrieks.

---

*If you want to stay put, turn to page 52.*

*Or, join Annie on page 13.*

# 34

You can't leave Annie behind. You charge forward and butt one of the creatures holding her with the hard point of your Magic Marker hat.

"Take that!" you shout as the creature falls down. Annie bites the arm of the other beast, who shrieks and lets her go. She scrambles toward you.

Another creature grabs your arm, but you hardly feel its claws slashing your skin. You whip your arm around, and it loses its grip, flying into a few others and knocking them down. You see an opening in the howling mob that leads to a door. Grabbing Annie's hand, you head for it.

But before you reach the door, it flies open. A gigantic creature stands in the doorway. It moves forward, and you back away.

It's twice as tall as the others—twice as tall as you—and covered with black fur. Its ugly smile reveals needle-sharp fangs. Its red eyes gleam, and drool drips from one corner of its mouth. It smells gross. Its breathing comes out in a low, steady growl.

*Eww! Turn to page 75.*

As the first kid slimes your face, the second kid turns away. When he turns back, his human face is gone! Instead, you see a hideous head with bright red eyes and a grinning mouth full of fangs. In the creature's hand is a mask . . . a mask of your face!

The creature pulls on your "face." "That's all right!" says another kid.

Your face smiles at you from the monster's head. "Okay! Time to go home, or Mom and Dad will be worried. Hey, I hope I like your mom and dad. Well, it's only for a year . . . unless they're really cool. Then I'll stick around."

The kid you first met hands you something floppy and rubbery. It's the face the other kid has just taken off.

"If I were you, I'd put this on," the "kid" says. "Right now, you look sort of gross."

The strangers walk away, laughing.

You stand there, stunned. What are you going to do? They've stolen your family. Your whole life. Your face!

Two kids in pirate costumes walk by and glance at you. One of them screams. The other one shakes his head in admiration.

"That's the ugliest mask I ever saw," he says.

**The End**

# 36

"Who's coming?" the old man asks, looking outside. "Friends of yours?"

"No!" you say. "They're vampires!"

The old man turns away from the door. "Vampires!" he says. "You wouldn't try to kid an old man, would you?"

"It's the truth," Annie says. "They're after us!"

"Henry, we have to help these children!" exclaims the old woman.

"You're right, Martha." Henry darts behind the counter. "Where did we put those stakes?"

The old couple seems energized.

"Under the cash register, dear. I'll get them." She hurries behind the counter and pulls out a bundle of sticks trimmed to sharp points and a heavy hammer.

The old man smiles. "That'll do it. Let's give those nasty vampires a Halloween surprise. You kids stay put and don't get in our way. Everything'll be fine."

The front door opens. The head vampire stands there. You and Annie tremble with fear. Can these old people really help?

*Find out on page 48.*

You and Annie jump down from the tailgate of the truck . . . and find yourselves in the middle of a ring of vampires. The driver of the truck also sports a pair of fangs.

"The groceries are here!" he says to the other vampires. "Come and get them! I even got some extra treats on the way!"

Two vampires leap onto the truck and pick up the "packages"—people tied up with gags in their mouths. One of them is Timmy!

He tries to say something just as he's grabbed by a vampire in the truck. But he's quickly thrown down to a thirsty vampire below, who laughs and tosses him over her shoulder. "It's *party time*! Happy Halloween!"

You turn to run but powerful arms grab you from behind. It's the head vampire, whom you last saw at the end of the tunnel!

"But . . . you . . . I saw you . . ."

"We can fly, you know," he says. "You'd be amazed how fast we can get from place to place as bats. But you'll be learning all about us, very soon. You'll be one of us."

He joins the other vampires, each one carrying a tied-up bundle from the truck. They spread out to enjoy their holiday feast . . . *you!*

**The End**

# 38

"Shut up!" Annie whispers. When a floor-board squeaks, you nearly scream.

"Okay," you say. "We're in the house. Hooray for us. Now let's get out and—"

"O-o-h!" A weird howl from somewhere above you echoes through the room. "O-o-h! No-o-o-oh!"

You're too scared to move.

"No-o-o-oh . . . AGHH!" The howl becomes a scream. Then the scream is suddenly cut off.

"What was that?" Annie's voice trembles.

"A scream," you whisper. "From upstairs."

Thump. Thump. Thump.

"Are those footsteps?" Annie eyes the stair-case.

"Yeah," whispers Jeff. "Heavy ones. They're moving!"

Thump. Thump. Thump.

The steps get louder. The walls seem to shake. "They're coming down the stairs," Annie whispers. Just then, Jeff's flashlight flickers—and goes out!

"Let's get out of here!" you shout. You start to run but trip on the edge of a rug and flop on the floor. Annie falls down next to you.

*Turn to page 11.*

"Oh, really?" you say. "Would you rather be back there with those ghosts with the axes?"

You notice Annie talking to a woman you don't know. Her floor-length dress and long hair are jet black, and her face is very pale. Her name tag says MS. VENNER.

"Wow! That's great makeup she's got," you say. "She looks like a real vampire."

"Yeah, I guess," Jeff says.

Annie turns as you come up. "This is Ms. Venner," she says, introducing you and Jeff. "She says there's a fun house down the hall called the Ghoul Room. Want to check it out? Ms. Venner says it's awesome."

"Okay," Jeff says. "Maybe some other kids want to go, too." He looks around the cafeteria.

"No!" Ms. Venner says. "I mean, most people have gone through it already. It's more fun to go a few at a time. Why don't you three give it a try?" She winks. "Unless you're too scared."

"I'm not scared," you say. "It sounds cool. They've never done anything like this before."

"No," says Ms. Venner. "This is the first time."

---

*Enter the Ghoul Room on page 51.*

"Yeah, those things clawed and bit me at the pond," says Jeff. "But I'll be okay. The thing is, I'm really *hungry.*"

He stares at you, a funny look on his face. His *mouth* looks weird all of a sudden. His lips are bulging outward. Something seems to be happening to his body, too—it's getting *thicker.* And is that *hair* on the backs of his hands?

"The bites will heal," Jeff says. His voice is deeper. He steps toward you but keeps himself between you and the doors.

"It's lucky we got away from those monsters," he says. He licks his lips. His teeth have grown long and needle-sharp! He raises his arms, and you see his fingernails are growing longer and more pointed as you watch. You scan the garage for another way out, but there isn't any.

"If we hadn't escaped," Jeff says, advancing toward you, "I'd have had to share you. Now, I can have you all to myself!"

You start to scream, but your scream is cut off as Jeff's fangs sink deep into your throat.

**The End**

# 42

The second ghoul corners Jeff. Quickly, you spray the ghoul with white stuff from the fire extinguisher. Jeff escapes. But now the extinguisher is empty!

You throw it at the ghoul and dodge under its outstretched arms.

"A fire alarm!" Jeff yells, pointing to a red box nearby. "I'm going to set it off."

"You shouldn't do that," Annie calls out.

"Yeah, but I don't see a 'ghoul alarm' anywhere," you say. "Do it, Jeff!"

Jeff jerks the handle on the red box. You hear a loud ringing. The ghouls stop and go back through the door they used to come in.

A moment later, the boiler room door opens. Ms. Venner stands there with an angry-looking janitor holding a big bunch of keys.

"What are you kids doing?" he demands. This place is off-limits! And so are fire alarms!"

"These ghouls wanted to eat us!" Annie explains.

Ms. Venner and the janitor stare at her.

*Think they believe Annie? Turn to page 27.*

He stops talking. The man-wolf wades into the water! It *can* swim! And it's coming straight at you!

"Can't you row faster?" wails Annie.

You're rowing as hard as you can, but you try to speed up. It doesn't matter. The man-wolf is faster.

"We'll never make it to the island!" Jeff yells.

"It doesn't matter if we do," Jordan gasps. "That thing will be waiting for us when we get there!"

The man-wolf is only a few yards away. You're out of breath and ready to give up. Suddenly the water around the creature begins to churn and bubble. The beast stops swimming and lets out a roar. It disappears under the water!

"What's happening? Where'd it go?" Jeff asks.

Abruptly a huge head breaks the water's surface, the man-wolf held tightly in its mouth. The man-wolf squeals and is dragged under again. It doesn't come back.

*Turn to page 86.*

## 44

"You mean the Caswell house is h-h-h—?" Annie is having trouble even saying the word.

"*Haunted*. That's right." Jeff looks serious.

"No way!" you say. "There's no such thing as a haunted house."

"I knew you'd chicken out." Jeff grins. "I'll go check it out while you go trick-or-treating."

"I'm not chicken!" you say. "I'll go."

"Me too, I guess," Annie says unhappily.

The Caswell house sits alone on a dead-end street. It is dark and silent. The front porch creaks under your feet as you step onto it.

Jeff pulls a flashlight from his pocket and switches it on. "Everyone ready? Let's do it."

He pulls the front door open and heads inside. The damp, chilly house is filled with dusty old furniture. You know that if you panic and run, Jeff will tease you about it for the rest of your life.

"Rumor has it the sons' ghosts show up every Halloween," Jeff says softly. "Sometimes their parents' ghosts show up, too. Maybe we'll see them."

*Will you? Go to page 38.*

"Fred! Here, boy! Where *is* that dog?" says a woman.

"I told you the dog needs training!" a man replies. "We should send him to obedience school. *Fred!* Come here!"

"Should we kill them, too?" asks a male witch.

"No, you fool!" Ms. Venner snaps. "If we kill too many, we'll be hunted, and maybe caught. We can't let these adults find us. We have to let the children go. Quickly!"

The witches loosen their grip. As you stand up, you stare at the witches. Something weird is happening to them!

Their faces are changing! Ms. Venner looks younger and more normal. The others change, too. A few look familiar.

Annie gasps. "Mr. Scott! Our gym teacher!"

You recognize Mr. Scott and a few other teachers. Even the assistant principal!

Except for Ms. Venner, they're all from your school!

"We can't let these kids go," the assistant principal worries. "They've seen who we really are! They'll tell!"

*Turn to page 85.*

## 46

As you run, you don't see any kids. The houses you pass are dark and empty. You wish you'd said no to the party. But it's too late to turn back. You're totally lost. How do these kids run so fast for so long? you wonder.

You reach a corner, lit by a lone streetlight. "We're here!" Marty says.

In front of you is a house, its windows lit up. You hear music.

"All right!" gasps Annie, who is seriously out of breath.

"I hope we can find our way home," you say.

"Don't worry about that," says one of the kids.

"I guess they don't have to worry about making too much noise," you tell Annie.

"That's right!" Marty says, opening the door. "We can make all the noise we want. No one can hear us."

"And no one complains," says another one.

Inside, the noise is deafening. There are more kids in the same furry outfits. You don't see Jeff, but it's a big house.

"Where's the food?" asks Annie.

A voice calls, "It just got here!"

---

*Huh? Turn to page 65.*

"What'll we do?" Jeff asks.

You have an idea. "This way!"

You race up a driveway, where an empty garage stands with its door open. "We'll hide in here until they go past."

Jeff hurries in. On a shelf you find a flashlight. You turn it on as Jeff swings the garage doors shut.

"Turn off the light!" he hisses. "They'll see it!"

You snap it off and stand in the dark with Jeff. The howls get louder. And louder.

Now the howls are right outside the garage! You force yourself to stay quiet and not move. The howls get softer. The beasts are moving away. They're gone! They didn't find you! You sigh with relief.

You switch on the flashlight and grin at Jeff. "Let's get out of here!"

But Jeff doesn't move. "Not yet," he says. He takes off his coat and drops it on the floor. Under his torn shirt, you see gashes and bites on his arms and body. He's bleeding!

"You need a doctor!" you exclaim, peering at the wounds.

*Learn the truth on page 41.*

# 48

The vampire steps inside, and the old man knocks him flat on his back. Quickly the old woman leaps up on him, places the stake point against his chest, and hammers it into his heart. The vampire shrieks and collapses like a torn balloon. A few seconds later, there's nothing left but his clothes and a little puddle of goo. The old woman jumps to her feet. "Next," she says.

A second vampire enters, is knocked down, and gets staked. She melts, too. The other vampires in the doorway turn back into bats and flap away.

"There!" says the old woman. "You won't have any more trouble from those nasty things."

The old man grins. "That was fun! Too bad Halloween happens only once a year!"

"You've done this before?" you ask.

"Sure!" says the man. "We've been killing vampires every Halloween for fifty years now."

The old woman sighs. "There aren't as many as there used to be."

As Henry gets a mop, Martha gets out the pumpkin pie. "Before we drive you kids home, how about some pumpkin pie?"

**The End**

"It's probably not a wolf at all," Jordan argues.

"Right," says Timmy. "It might be another big bloodthirsty animal. Or a werewolf."

"I say we keep going," Jordan insists. "Jeff needs us."

"Let's stay together," you say. "We'll probably scare whatever it is away."

"Right," Timmy agrees. "Make lots of noise."

You start walking again. Everyone begins to shout, cough, and stomp the ground as loud as they can.

At the head of the line, Timmy stops suddenly. Everyone crashes into each other.

"I see a light!" he says.

You and the others peer into the darkness. You see a flickering gleam, like a candle, through a gap in the trees.

Then you hear another howl.

You fight the urge to turn and run as fast as you can. Instead, you keep walking toward the light, which gets brighter as you get closer.

*Y-A-A-A-O-O-O-H-H-H-R-R-R-H!*

*Walk to page 72.*

You, Annie, and Jeff follow Ms. Venner down the hall. At the end of the hall Ms. Venner starts down the stairs.

"The Ghoul Room is in the basement?" asks Annie.

"That's right," Ms. Venner says. "We couldn't get a room upstairs to use. It's right this way."

It's very quiet at the bottom of the stairs. You can't hear the music, screams, and laughter. "I don't see any kids or teachers," whispers Jeff.

"Most of them went to the Ghoul Room earlier," you point out. "While we were in the haunted house."

"Here we are," Ms. Venner says, stopping in front of a door with a frosted glass window. You can't see what's inside, but a dim light shines through. She opens the door and steps aside to let you in. "Have fun! Happy Halloween!"

You go in. The door closes behind you. Nobody's here. There are no decorations. Two dim ceiling lamps give off a little light. Machines hum quietly.

*Are you in the right place? Turn to page 59.*

## 52

As you crouch under the table, the grinning face of the ghost appears near you. "You think you can hide from me?" it says. "Guess again!"

It reaches out a ghostly hand to grab you, but you squirm away and crawl from under the table. The ghost *floats* over the table, straight at you!

*"Over here!"* Annie shouts. You dash through an open door. You're out of the house! A second later, Jeff dives through a window. Behind him, you see the young man's pale, ghostly face. You run away from the house as fast as you can. You don't stop until you can't run another step.

The three of you stand under a streetlight, panting. "Great idea, Jeff. Brilliant!" Annie huffs.

You nod. "I have more fun at the dentist's."

"I'm the one who almost got killed in there," Jeff points out. "Remember?"

"What'll we do now?" you ask.

*Turn to page 14.*

You huddle against the wall farthest from the door. With a slam, the door flies open. Something leaps into the shack. You catch a glimpse of dirty gray fur and a whiff of an awful smell before you squeeze your eyes tightly shut.

Annie grabs your hand. You wonder who will die first. You keep your eyes closed, not wanting to see what is in the shack with you.

*R-R-R-R-H-H-H-R-R-R!*

As you hear the growl, Annie's hand is jerked out of yours.

"No!" she screams. Then silence.

You cautiously open your eyes. Jeff is crouching on the floor. Jordan stares back at you.

The huge furry thing is gone.

So is Annie.

---

*Is Annie a werewolf snack? Turn to page 62.*

# 54

"We'll find something," you say as you hunt through the junk, looking for anything you can use as a weapon. A machine gun might do it, or a tank. But you won't find a tank here.

*Crash!* The snarling is suddenly louder. You and Annie stare at each other in fear. The creatures have broken down the door!

You spot something behind a stack of beach chairs. "This may be just what we need." You start tossing the chairs aside.

*"Beach chairs?"* Annie screams.

You pull out a beach umbrella, folded around its pole. The pole comes to a sharp point.

"Hold this with me," you order. The two of you take the umbrella and hold it with the point facing out. You blow out the candle and stand at the head of the stairs.

You hear a nasty growl. Heavy footsteps start up the steps. You can see the outline of a huge creature coming upward, getting closer. Its lips are pulled back in a snarl. Behind it are dozens of the other beasts.

All eager for a mouthful of you and Annie.

"Wait for my signal," you whisper.

---

*Charge back to page 20.*

"We'd be okay on that island," says Jeff.

"How do we get there?" you ask. "Swimming in this stuff may be as dangerous as that wolf-thing." The pond stinks from the toxic chemicals dumped here.

"There's a boat!" Jeff shouts.

*A-A-H-H-H-H-R-R-O-O-O-H-R!*

"It's coming!" you say. "Hurry!"

You help Jeff drag the boat into the dark, smelly pond. It's big enough for all of you. There are oars in it, and you know how to row.

There's another roar from the woods.

"It's coming!" you cry.

---

*Ready for a boat trip? Turn to page 84.*

# 56

Soon you're at the edge of thick, dark woods. You hear strange noises. One may be an owl. But what's that howling?

"Are there wolves around here?" asks Annie.

*"Wolves?"* Jordan looks disgusted. "Get real!"

"Here's a trail!" calls Timmy. "Hurry up!"

You proceed single file between big trees. From the bushes, you hear crackling and crunching. It sounds as if an animal is in the underbrush. A very large animal.

"Where's the pond?" Jordan grumbles.

"It's not far," says Timmy. "We're nearly there, I think."

"Well, we better get there soon," Annie warns, "or—"

*"AWO-O-O-O-H!"*

It's that howling again! This time it sounds louder and closer. Everyone stops.

"No wolves, huh?" Annie swings her flashlight around. "Something's doing a pretty good imitation. Let's get out of here!"

"Maybe she's right," says Timmy.

"We have to find Jeff!" Jordan insists.

You try to decide what to do.

---

*Want to go back? Turn to page 82.*

*If you have the guts to keep going, turn to page 49.*

"Poor you. Trapped. With no place to run." He licks his lips. "One bite and you too will become vampires and join our hunt for blood."

Impulsively you aim your flashlight at his face. It's much brighter than Annie's. When the beam hits him, he twists away.

"Turn that off!" he screams.

You keep him blinded with your flashlight, so he can't move. But the other vampires are getting closer.

You move your flashlight to an advancing vampire. Dazzled, she freezes in place. You realize you can slow the vampires by moving your flashlight back and forth among them. But sooner or later, they're bound to get you.

*Turn to page 87.*

Annie's eyes grow big. "Graystone Pond? You want to go there now? At night?"

"Jeff's our friend, right?" asks Timmy.

Annie shakes her head. "He's not *that* much of a friend!"

"Chicken! I'll go," Jordan says, glaring at Annie. She has a crush on Jeff.

"Not me," says Annie. "I'd get in trouble."

They all look at you.

"How about it?" Timmy asks you. "You coming or not?"

---

*If you agree to go look for Jeff, turn to page 24.*

*If going to the pond at night sounds crazy, turn to page 66.*

"*This* is the Ghoul Room?" asks Jeff, looking disgusted. "Give me a break!"

You look at the machines. "It's the boiler room. These are furnaces. Ms. Venner brought us to the wrong place."

Jeff goes to the door and twists the knob. It won't turn. He twists harder. You're locked in. "Great," he snaps.

Annie hammers on the door. "Help! Hey!"

"Nobody'll hear you upstairs," you say.

"Was Ms. Venner a teacher of yours?" Jeff asks Annie.

She shakes her head. "I never saw her before. I guess she's new."

You look around. Metal stairs lead to an upstairs catwalk. There are narrow windows up there. Behind the furnaces you spot a door.

"Maybe that door isn't locked," you say, going to see. Before you get there, the door opens. A man is standing there. Annie runs over.

"Boy, are we glad to see—"

The man grabs Annie by the throat!

*What is his problem? Turn to page 26.*

Suddenly the trail ends. The "lights" are actually candlelit jack-o'-lanterns set here and there on the hill. They're carved in ugly faces.

There's a flapping noise overhead. Annie shrieks. Dark shapes flitter all around, and something leathery brushes your face. You hear a lot of high-pitched squeaking.

"I hate bats!" Timmy yells. "They're ugly!"

"What a nasty thing to say," says a grown-up voice.

A tall, thin man stands by the jack-o'-lanterns. "I like bats," he says. "My best friends are bats. We're celebrating."

"Celebrating?" Timmy repeats.

"Yes," the man says. "It's Halloween. And there's a full moon. It's a very special night."

"Um, I think we'd better get going," you say, sensing something weird about this guy.

"What's your hurry?" the man asks.

To your horror, a few bats land, grow larger—and take human shapes! Timmy shrieks and runs for the woods. You and Annie are frozen in place with fear.

Up on the hillside, you spot the mouth of a cave. It's not too far away!

---

*If you want to head for the woods, turn to page 67.*

*If you think the cave is safer, turn to page 79.*

"Quick!" says Jordan. "Let's go before that thing comes back!"

She starts to run, but a furry arm reaches out from behind the doorway and lifts her off the ground. She shrieks. So do you.

*"SHUT UP!"* roars a voice. A tall, thin man in smelly furs stands there. His gray hair and beard are dirty. He sets Jordan down, glaring. It's the hermit!

"Scared you, huh? Serves you right, bothering a man in his home!"

"That was you doing all that howling?" Jordan asks, brushing herself off.

"R-R-R-Right!" he growls.

"Why do you live out here?" Jeff asks.

"Don't like people," the man snarls.

"What did you do with Annie?" you ask.

"That girl? I tossed her in the bushes. Now get out, before I toss you on the fire!"

"You wouldn't do that!" you say.

He grins, showing a lot of long yellow teeth. "Want to stay around to see?"

No one does. You leave. Fast.

**The End**

You're in an open field, with a road nearby. You spot a roadside diner, decorated for Halloween.

"Where are we?" Annie asks, looking around.

You shrug. "We can't be far from home. I bet if we ask people at that diner, we can—"

"Hello!" A vampire head pops out of the tunnel opening. "You didn't think we'd give up, did you? Not on Halloween!"

*"Run!"* you yell. You take off as fast as your feet can carry you toward the road. "Head for the diner!"

A truck is barreling down the road. "Let's stop it!" Annie shrieks.

"What if they don't stop?" you shout back. "Head for the diner! There are people inside!"

"But the truck can get us out of here!" Annie cries.

---

*If you think stopping the truck makes sense, turn to page 25.*

*If you think the diner doesn't serve vampires, turn to page 70.*

# 64

"You're a total moron!" Timmy says. "We came out here because we thought you were in trouble!"

Jeff sulks. "I didn't ask you to."

"Who are you trying to scare?" you ask. "The owls?"

"The guy who lives there." Jeff points to the shack.

"Somebody lives out *here*?" asks Annie.

Jeff nods. "Yeah, a hermit. And I bet I've got him scared stiff by now."

"Why do you want to scare him?" you ask. "Did he ever do anything to you?"

"No," Jeff admits.

Annie shakes her head. "Let's get out of here."

"Good idea," Timmy says.

Everyone except Jeff turns to go.

"Hey!" Jeff calls. "Don't you want to stick around until the hermit panics and runs?"

"No," you say, walking away. Then you hear another *YA-A-A-A-W-O-O-H-R-R-H!*

Now you're really mad. You spin around. "Jeff, turn that stupid tape off! It's not funny!"

---

*Stop Jeff's laughter on page 8.*

The door slams behind you with a loud crash. Suddenly all the lights go out.

You hear growling near you. Something rough brushes your face, and you jerk away.

Someone lights a candle. In the glow of the candlelight, you see that you and Annie are surrounded by kids in furry costumes. . . .

Then you look closer and see they're *not* wearing costumes. Or gloves. Or masks. They're not *kids.* The fangs in their drooling mouths are real. They begin to close in on you, and their growling gets louder. They cast weird shadows in the candlelight.

Suddenly a pair of ugly claws takes a swipe at you. You jerk back. The claws barely miss you, leaving four rips in your costume.

"Let's get out of here!" you yell to Annie, as you run for the door.

But the creatures swarm around you, and you're cut off. "Leaving already?" one of them spits. "The party's just getting started."

"What . . . what *are* you?" Annie whispers.

"You want to know what we are?" it snarls. "I'll tell you. We are *hungry!*"

---

*Is this the kind of party you had in mind?*
*Turn to page 4.*

You feel bad as you watch Timmy and Jordan walk away. But not bad enough to run after them.

"Hey! Have you seen Jeff Farrell?" Annie asks a group of kids walking down the street.

"What's he dressed as?" asks a big kid in a Frankenstein costume.

"Um . . . we don't know," you answer.

"So how do we know if we've seen him?" asks Frankenstein. His friends laugh. Embarrassed, you and Annie walk quickly away.

"Let's ask this group," you say, pointing to six kids coming around the corner.

The new kids look about your age, but you can't be sure. They're covered from head to foot in furry costumes. They wear gloves with claws and animal masks.

"Those are awesome outfits," Annie says.

You agree. "They must be hot, though," you whisper.

"Hey, have you guys seen Jeff?" you ask.

The fur kids look at each other.

"Who?" one of them says. You don't recognize the voice.

*Go to page 6.*

You don't want to get trapped in the cave, so you turn and run as fast as you can after Timmy. Annie is close behind you. The vampires chase you along the trail, with the real bats darting and squeaking alongside you.

The vampires are gaining!

Annie trips and falls. You grab her arm. "Come on! We've got to hurry!"

But you've been slowed down . . . and the vampires are catching up.

Two vampires burst onto the trail in front of you, cutting you off. Behind you are three others, including the one who spoke to you in the first place.

"That was a fine chase," he says, licking his lips. "Exercise works up a good appetite."

*A-A-A-A-O-O-O-R-R-R-G-H!*

It's the howl of the werewolf again—not far away!

*Race to page 76.*

You continue to use your flashlight to slow the vampires down. Annie shines her light to see where you're going, while you watch the vampires.

Without warning, Annie stops. "Watch out!"

You freeze. Annie's light shines down into a hole. You move slowly around the hole, but one of the vampires falls in.

"That's one gone," you tell Annie.

But wait. The vampire isn't dead. Instead, it turns back into a bat and flies out of the hole. To your horror, it takes back its human shape and comes after you.

You move as quickly as you can. "Take your time!" the head vampire calls out to his cronies. "We'll get them sooner or later."

But the cave floor ends where you stand. In front of you is a giant hole. The vampires laugh. There's nowhere for you to go.

Annie grabs your hand. Which is worse? If the vampires catch you and drink your blood, you'll turn into vampires like them. Your only other choice is to jump into the pit.

The vampires are getting close. You'd better make up your minds quickly!

CRUNCH! Oops. Too late!

**The End**

The ghost near Jeff grins. "Go ahead, brother," it tells the other ghost. "It's your turn to kill."

What?

You hope this is some kind of nightmare.

But it's not.

You turn to see the ghost behind you raise its ax.

"Prepare to die!" cries the ghost.

*"No!"* Annie shouts. She runs forward and butts the ghost with her shoulder.

You expect to see Annie fall right through it—after all, it's a ghost—but instead, the ghost drops its ax. *"Uuumpph!"*

Encouraged by this development, you ram the other ghost from behind.

*"Whooof!"* The other ghost falls on top of Jeff's body, the blood bucket sloshing all over the floor.

*"Ow!"* says Jeff's corpse. "That hurt!"

"Jeff!" you exclaim. "Are you still alive?"

"It sure looks like it," Annie says. You notice that Annie is glowing, just like the ghosts.

*What's going on? Find out on page 74.*

# 70

You sprint toward the diner. "I can't tell if it's open!"

"The sign says OPEN," Annie gasps. She is nearly out of breath. But she keeps going. The vampires are hot on your trail.

The diner's windows are painted with brightly colored Halloween images: big orange jack-o'-lanterns with friendly smiles, witches on broomsticks, a funny-looking Frankenstein monster. A paper sign above the front door reads HAPPY HALLOWEEN! You yank open the door, burst inside, and look around.

The place is empty. There are no customers. Sitting at a stool in front of the counter is an old woman in a faded waitress uniform. She swivels to face you. She doesn't look as if she'd be much help in a fight with a full-grown vampire. The only other person in the place is an old man in a cook's apron behind the counter, polishing a glass with a dishrag.

The old woman gets slowly to her feet. "Hello, children," she says in a thin, trembly voice. "Happy Halloween!"

*Can they help you? Go to page 15.*

# 72

This time the howl comes from *behind* you. You grit your teeth and keep going.

"Hold it!" whispers Timmy. "Take a look at this!" He crouches behind some bushes surrounding a clearing in the woods. The full moon shines down brightly on the open space. In the middle of the clearing you see a small shack built out of pieces of scrap wood. The roof is made of shingles, and a shiny metal pipe chimney sticks through it. The door is made of rough, unpainted planks. Next to the doorway, hanging from a nail, is a lantern. Its flame is the light you saw.

You hear howling again, but now it's somewhere to one side of you.

"*Shhh!* I hear footsteps!" Timmy says.

You can hear them, too. *Loud* footsteps. Something is crashing through the bushes near you. And getting closer.

Annie shuts her eyes. "I wish I were in bed with the covers pulled over my head. I wish I were anyplace but here. I wish—"

"Cut it out!" Jordan says. "You're giving *me* the creeps."

*Go to page 12.*

You dash outside. Behind you, the beasts howl in anger. Annie calls your name. You run down the block and around the corner, looking over your shoulder as you go.

There's nothing following you, yet. You stop to figure out where you are.

"Psst! *Hey!*" says a voice from the bushes by the side of the street. You freeze, ready to run if it's another monster.

But it's Jeff Farrell! His face is pale, and his clothes are torn and dirty.

*"What are you doing here?"* you yell. "Everybody's looking for you! What hap—"

"Shhh!" Jeff shakes his head and flaps his arms. *"Shut up,* or those things'll hear you! They're not kidding about eating you. They're for real."

You lower your voice. "What do you know about them? Where have you been?"

"After school I went to Graystone Pond to hang out. This bunch of fur-covered creeps jumped me and took me to that house. I couldn't get away. There were too many of them. Then one creep ordered the rest to lock me in the cellar until later."

---

*Turn to page 9.*

You look down at yourself. You're glowing, too! Then you squint at a heavy curtain pulled along one wall. "I think I know what's happening. Come here and take a look."

You draw the curtain aside. Behind it shines a light with a purple cast. Under the glow, you and Annie have the same ghost-shine.

"It's 'black light,'" you explain. "It makes things shine and look weird, like these ghosts."

The ghost who fell on Jeff stands up. He shrugs and looks embarrassed.

"It wasn't my idea," he says. His voice sounds normal now. "Jeff thought it up."

"Turn on the lights," says the other ghost, picking up the ax he dropped. "The joke's over, I guess."

"*Joke?*" Annie repeats, looking at the ghosts and Jeff. "Some joke! I was scared to death!"

As the lights go on, Jeff gets up. He's covered from head to foot with "blood." He glares at the "ghost" who fell on him.

"You should have watched where you were going," he says angrily. "Now I have this stuff all over me!"

*Turn to page 23.*

"What's going on here?" it says in a deep, rumbling voice. Its red eyes stare into yours. You look away. "Have you been fighting? Don't you know how to behave at a party?" It licks its lips with a long pink tongue and raises two paws armed with vicious claws. "We're going to have to punish you."

In total panic, you search wildly for an escape, but you're surrounded. The hairy monster lunges forward and squeezes you in its powerful arms. You struggle, but it's too strong. You can't breathe. You feel your body getting weaker. It's going to strangle you! There's nothing you can do to stop it!

Suddenly it lets out a howl and drops you on the floor. It whirls and glares at Annie. She has an opened safety pin in her hand. You realize that she must have taken it from her costume and pricked the monster.

The monster lets out an angry roar and reaches for Annie. Quickly you grab a lit candle from one of the creatures and hold the flame against the giant monster's leg. Yes! Its fur catches on fire. It howls in agony, whirling toward you. You and Annie break for the door.

*Turn to page 83.*

The vampires look around, confused.

Footsteps crash through the bushes.

Out of the trees comes . . . *Jordan!* She's alive! She holds up a long braid of garlic. The vampires back away.

"Take that away!" screams the head vampire.

*A-A-A-R-R-R-O-O-O-O-G-H!*

The howl is very loud. Two vampires flee. Behind the head vampire, Jeff appears with more garlic.

The other vampires vanish into the trees.

Annie hugs Jeff. "You saved our lives!"

You hug Jordan. "We thought the werewolf got you!"

"Werewolf?" Jordan asks. "What werewolf?"

"The one that's been howling ever since we got here!" you reply.

Jordan grins. "That was no werewolf. That was Jeff."

Jeff cups his hand to his mouth. *"YA-A-A-A-O-O-O-O . . ."*

"Wow. You're good at that," Annie says.

Jeff smiles. "Thanks! I've been practicing."

**The End**

"Forget it," you reply. "Let's go trick-or-treating."

"But I'm covered with this goo!" Jeff protests.

As you try to find something to clean Jeff off, a door creaks open behind him. Two young men stand in a closet doorway. One holds an ax and the other wields a knife. Their skin is greenish and they smell horrible.

"Are they part of the joke?" Annie whispers.

"N-n-no!" Joey stammers. "They must be the real Cas . . . Cas—"

*"Caswells,"* says one of the men in a weird, echoey voice. They grab Jeff's shoulders and drag him backward. Jeff can't get loose.

"Help!" he yells.

One of the Caswells glares at you, then shows you his knife. *"Go,"* he says. *"Now."*

You all rush out as Jeff is pulled, screaming, into the closet.

Outside, Joey turns to Ernie. "How are we going to get Dad to sell the house now?"

**The End**

# 78

"I don't really feel like any more trick-or-treating," you say. "I'm too tired." You say good-bye to your friends and head home.

You start walking. "Hey!" calls a voice from behind you. It's the kid who asked you to go trick-or-treating. He and his friends run in your direction.

They spread out in a circle around you.

"I'd better go," you say. "It's late."

"No it's not," says a second kid.

"It's early," says the first one.

You look around for help, but there's nobody to be seen. It's just you and these weird kids.

"What do you think?" the first kid asks the second. "Will this one be all right?"

The second kid studies you. "Sure. I'm tired of this mask. I've been wearing it a whole year."

Mask?

Two of the kids grab your arms. The first one spreads horrible-smelling slime on your face. You can't yell, or even move!

*Turn to page 35.*

You and Annie dash toward the cave. You don't dare look to see if the vampires are following you.

You have to duck to get inside the cave, but once you're in, you can stand. In fact, the cave is so big, your footsteps echo and the beam of your powerful flashlight won't even reach the ceiling.

Annie shines her flashlight around. "Wow!" Her voice echoes off the cave walls.

You hear leathery flapping and shrill squeaking. There are a lot of bats around here. Annie crouches down in fear.

"Annie, don't worry about the bats," you say, trying to remain calm. "They only eat bugs and fruit. They won't hurt us."

But something else will.

"They went in here!" shrieks a voice just outside the cave. It's the vampire leader. A moment later, you hear his footsteps inside the cave. Other vampires come in, too. Annie's flashlight lights up the first one's face. He smiles, showing his needle-sharp fangs.

*Hurry to page 57!*

# 80

Your hand closes on another hand, and you squeeze it as hard as you can.

"Take it easy!" says a voice. The person jumps off you. You whirl around. It's Jeff!

He smirks. "Scared you!" he says.

"Very funny . . . *not*," you say. "Your mom and dad are going crazy wondering where you are. And Timmy and Jordan were so worried, they went to Graystone Pond to look for you."

Jeff pouts. "*I* didn't ask them to go there. It's not *my* fault." He laughs. "Look at you guys, trick-or-treating like little babies! *Boring!*"

"You have a better idea?" Annie snaps.

"Yeah," Jeff replies. "But it's too scary for you dweebs." He starts walking, leaving the two of you to catch up.

"Where are you going?" you call.

Jeff looks over his shoulder. "To the Caswell house."

"Is there a party there?" Annie asks.

Jeff laughs. "No one lives there. The Caswells are dead. Their crazy sons killed them with axes. They say you can hear the Caswells screaming in the upstairs rooms late at night."

*Turn to page 44 if you dare.*

The three of you clatter up the steps. The ghouls follow, but you drive them back with a squirt from the fire extinguisher. "Take that!" you yell, giving the trigger a sharp pull. *Phhht.* The white stuff stops. It's empty.

You and Jeff boost Annie to the window handle. She yanks the window open, kneels on the ledge, and turns to help Jeff.

You hear the slow footsteps of the ghouls clanking up the stairs.

"Hurry!" you shriek, pushing Jeff as Annie pulls him. He gets to the ledge with Annie. They both reach down for you.

Out of the corner of your eye, you see the ghouls are at the top of the stairs. One lunges for your foot. Luckily, you swing yourself up on the ledge with the others in the nick of time.

"Let's get out of the Ghoul Room," Annie says, starting through the window.

"Excellent idea," Jeff says as he follows her. You're close behind.

---

*Are you safe? Turn to page 7.*

"I'm out of here!" Timmy announces.

"Me too!" Annie says. "I'm allergic to were-wolves."

"Me three," you say. "It's too weird!"

"Are you going to leave me here?" Jordan asks.

You shrug. "Make up your mind," you say.

Jordan puts on her stubborn-as-a-mule look. "I'm not going to leave Jeff here by himself!"

"Look," Timmy says, trying to persuade her. "If Jeff has gotten into trouble, he'll have to get out of it. Alone."

But Jordan shakes her head and starts walking away.

You and your friends follow Timmy down one of several trails. You hope it takes you out of the woods. And not into danger.

Suddenly you hear a scream. *Helllllp!*

"Jordan!" Annie cries, biting her lip.

You sigh. "I don't think we can help her . . . now."

"We'd better get going, or whatever got Jordan will come looking for us," Timmy gasps, starting down the trail.

"I see lights up ahead!" you exclaim.

*Is it a house? Go to page 60.*

Beyond the door you find a flight of stairs which you start to climb, stopping long enough to slam the door and lock it behind you. The two of you run up the steps, holding up the candle to light your way.

You find yourselves in a dusty attic, full of old furniture and junk. You hear pounding and snarls from the other side of the door as you head upward. The door won't keep them back for long.

"Maybe this'll keep them out," Annie says, struggling with a huge trunk. "Help me."

You put down the candle and help her drag the heavy trunk over and push it down the steps. It thuds against the door. You send an armchair and a dresser bumping after it. "That should slow them down, anyway," you say, looking around the attic.

Everything is covered with dust and cobwebs: boxes, lamps, birdcages, beach chairs. All the windows are barred with iron grills.

*Crack!* It sounds like the door has splintered! Annie peers down the stairs and gasps. "They'll be up here any minute, and there's nowhere to go! What are we going to do?"

*Hurry to page 54.*

## 84

Jeff, Jordan, and you jump into the boat, but Annie stays put.

"Come on, get in!" you yell at her.

"I'm not going near that water," she says. "It's toxic!"

There's another roar from the trees. It sounds closer.

"We're going!" yells Jeff. "If you want to come, get in!"

"Stay there and you'll be wolf meat!" Jordan shouts.

You're having second thoughts.

Should you stay in the boat? Or hop out and join Annie?

---

*If you stay in the boat, turn to page 32.*

*If you jump out, turn to page 88.*

Ms. Venner smiles evilly. "So? Who'll believe them? *'Help! Our teachers are all witches!'*"

She looks at you. "You're lucky . . . this time. You're safe . . . for now. But we'll be back. Maybe at the next full moon, or next Halloween."

With a toss of their heads, the teachers start walking back to the school.

You, Jeff, and Annie back up in the opposite direction.

From now on, you'll always participate in gym. You don't want to make Mr. Scott mad.

**The End**

You stop rowing and stare at the spot where the creature disappeared. A few bubbles float to the surface.

"What was that slimy thing?" Jordan asks.

"I don't know, but it was toxic," Annie answers.

"We've been saved by a monster!" Jeff says. He laughs. You all join in.

"Let's turn the boat around and go home," you say. "This has to be the wildest Halloween ever!"

"Too wild for me," Jordan says, shaking her head.

As you turn the boat, it starts to tilt.

"Annie, I told you to sit in the middle!" you yell.

"I *am* sitting in the middle!" says Annie.

The boat begins to rock back and forth.

"Then what—" Jeff starts.

Two gigantic, slimy tentacles pop out of the water and wrap around the boat. You start to scream. So does everyone else.

As the boat tips over and spills you into the smelly water, the last thing you see is a gigantic mouth full of sharp fangs, opening wide.

**The End**

"See where the cave goes while I hold them up!" you shout. Annie runs off.

"It goes way back!" she calls. "I can't see how far!" You hear her gasp. "I found something!"

You back away from the vampires toward the sound of Annie's voice. She's squatting by a branch of the cave, a much smaller one, like a tunnel.

"That's awfully small," you say. "I don't know. We might get stuck."

"Well, I'm scared of getting stuck in narrow places. I'd rather let the vampires get me."

You look back at the vampires. "They will," you say truthfully, "if we don't try this tunnel!"

---

*If you'll risk a tight squeeze, turn to page 5.*

*If you want to stick with Annie, turn to page 68.*

Annie waits as you leap out of the boat.

*"Hurry!"* she whispers.

You hear another roar. It's getting very close now. You turn to run and trip on a tree root. You fall in the dirt, hard. You feel dazed.

*"Come on!"* Annie orders. "What are you waiting for?"

"Okay," you gasp, slowly standing and rubbing the dirt from your eyes. You feel a hard nudge in your ribs.

"I'm coming! Cut it out!" you mutter.

There's a strong tug on your arm.

You're getting mad. "Annie, stop it! I've got something in my eyes!"

"Hurry!" Annie shouts. You realize that her voice is coming from far away. So how could her hand be on your arm?

You open your eyes and squint. It's not Annie's hand on your arm. It's a big, hairy paw, with long, needle-sharp claws.

You open your mouth to scream.

But nothing comes out.

**The End**